LITTLE PINK BOOK™

When Mom's Cancer Doesn't Go Away

Helping Children Cope with Loss and Beyond

Maryann Makekau

20/30north Studios

Visit www.thelittlepinkbooks.com for other Little Pink Book™ titles

All book titles will also be available in Spanish

1

For information, address:

Maryann Makekau

PO Box 2021

Fort Walton Beach, FL 32549

pinkbooks@cox.net

Set in Kristen ITC 12 point. Includes references.

A LITTLE PINK BOOK™ – When Mom's Cancer Doesn't Go Away: Helping Children Cope with Loss and Beyond. Library of Congress Cataloging (Pre-assigned Control Number)

Makekau, Maryann
ISBN-13: 978-0-9826601-1-9

ISBN-10: 0-98266-011-1

Note: The information in this book is true and complete to the best of our knowledge. This book is intended only as an informative guide for those wishing to know more about cancer issues. In no way is this book intended to replace, countermand or conflict with the advice given to you by your own physician. The ultimate decision concerning care should be made between you and your doctor. We strongly recommend you follow his or her advice. Information in this book is general and is offered with no guarantees on the part of the author or publisher. The author/publisher disclaims all liability in connection with use of this book.

 2

Foreword

Losing your mother to cancer is never easy, no matter what your age. But as a child, the loss is incomprehensible. The time together, special experiences and memories are much too abbreviated. But most difficult of all, is the loss of a mother's love, especially when you are far too young and need it most of all. When my mom died of breast cancer, I was 36 years old. It was her unconditional love I missed and grieved for the most. For a child, the loss of their mother's love, hugs, reassurance, and support is so tragic--it's impossible to grasp. But this is life. Each of us is born, and each of us will die. No matter how we wish it were different, some of us walk a shorter time on this earth than others. And some of those brief walkers are mothers with small children.

We, as adults try to make sense of the tragedies that are a part of life. For most of us, however, that is never easy, and sometimes even impossible to do. For a child, trying to make sense of and cope with the loss of your mother is unfathomable. Watching my own mother die from breast cancer, as well as taking care of disturbing numbers of young breast cancer patients (some in their 20's), impacted me so much that I left my plastic surgery practice to search for answers to the breast cancer epidemic.

I found them clearly laid out in the medical research: The American diet, lifestyle, and environment are a recipe for breast cancer (and prostate and colon cancer, heart disease, and poor health in general). That's actually good news; in most cases, something can be done to dramatically lower the risk. And for women who have breast cancer, research shows that making some simple changes in diet and lifestyle can radically improve the chances of living a long, healthy life. My life is now dedicated to teaching people about what they can do to achieve an extraordinary state of health and avoid getting deadly or debilitating chronic diseases. Prevention is a vital key in stopping the breast cancer epidemic and the tragic loss of so many lives.

3

However, sometimes no matter how well a person lives their life, they may be dealt the cards of cancer. And in some cases, no matter what a person does, that cancer doesn't go away. Maryann has done an extraordinary job dealing with a very difficult subject—one we all wish didn't exist. But it does.

As adults, it is our duty to prepare the children in our lives who are dealing with the impending loss of a parent as best we can. Our impulse may be to avoid such tough conversations with children, because they are just too difficult. We fear that we won't know the right words to say. That's why this book is so important. Maryann has provided an invaluable tool for those of us who know small children losing a parent to cancer. She has given us the right words to say and provided us with guidelines to help effectively support the grieving child.

Thank you, Maryann, for taking on this difficult task and for giving us the words that can make a difference.

Christin Horner, MD
Board certified surgeon and plastic surgeon
Author of *Waking the Warrior Goddess*
Winner of the IPPY award for "Best book in Health, Medicine and Nutrition" 2006

www.drchristinehorner.com

4

Dedication

This Little Pink Book™ serves to celebrate life, even in the midst of cancer taking it away. When Mom's Cancer Doesn't Go Away is dedicated to Bobbie Jo and Ed. Their love story carries courage to a new level. Justin, may you experience all the riches that special love has selflessly given to you. "And now these three remain: faith, hope and love. But the greatest of these is love." (1 Corinthians 13:13)

To Summer, Marlene and Jonathan—your mother's love remains in the fiber of your lives and her gentle touch is ever present.

This book is also dedicated to Jon and Maureen. As Maureen was losing her battle with cancer, she patiently taught Jon what moving on with life looks like. To my dear friends Vicki, Mari, Laurie and Julie who all lost their mothers to cancer. Their ability to carry on and later become tender-hearted mothers themselves is a testimony to love's eternal power. To all who lost the battle but left an indelible mark on our lives – you remain our compass: to value every gift whether big or small, to live life to the fullest, and to love in a way that envelopes the soul.

To Derek, thank you for another beautiful layout and stick-characters that bring optimism to life's toughest moments. Thank you, Chuck, for all your encouragement of this Little Pink Book™ series; your love is my anchor. To Loren, your all-encompassing heart for the little ones beams sunshine into my writing marathons. To Sam, your constant glowing spirit of "Samthusiasm" is a tremendous blessing to me. Thank you, Donna, Ruthie, Dorothy, Vicki and countless cheerleaders who tirelessly back me in this work. Thank you to all my family and friends for their wealth of support, encouragement and prayer for this series; I couldn't do this without any of you! Thank you, God for making me an instrument of your peace.

5

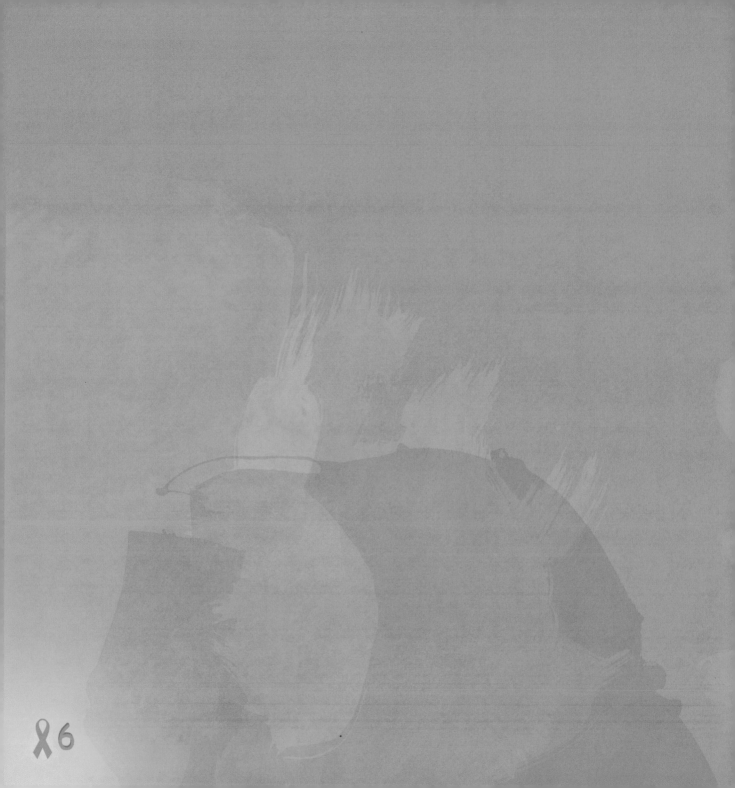

Table of Contents

Why Didn't Cancer Leave?

Cancer is a word that means disease. That means something went very wrong inside the body causing a person with it to get very sick. Cancer is also a word that a lot of people don't like to say. You might think that talking about cancer makes it real! It is real and that's what makes people afraid; cancer is not good because it hurts lives.

Some people get cancer and it stays for awhile, then it's gone. Other people get cancer that goes away, but then it comes back. Still other people get cancer that just doesn't go away. When cancer enters your family's life, it can make everyone feel confused. Cancer is a disease that changes a lot of things, especially when it doesn't go away. This book is about moms who have that kind of cancer, the kind that won't go away.

It might have started in her lungs or breasts and now it has shown up into other places, like in her brain or her bones. With that kind of cancer, the kind that doesn't go away, your mom isn't going to get better. Sometimes cancer takes life away, sometimes people die from cancer. Coping with that kind of loss is painful and confusing; and it can be very hard to understand all that's happening to your mom and to your family.

8

Changes at Home

When your mom gets sick with cancer, people may come together to help your family out. Grandmas, aunts, sisters, cousins and friends might come to visit and they might even stay for awhile. Cancer is really hard on everyone in the family, but you can help too. You can help by talking about your feelings, by doing chores and homework, by drawing pictures for mom, and by giving a hug to someone who's sad.

Your family may need to travel to a new place, to see a special doctor or go to a special hospital. After awhile you might get used to hearing about cancer and doctor visits, hospital trips and the many phone calls – everything seems to be about cancer.

Before cancer mom may have taken you to soccer games, surf lessons or piano practice. She may have played games with you and took you shopping. She may have helped you with your homework and listened when you had a problem with a friend. You might get angry and wish that life could be like it was before cancer.

Although your mom can probably still do some of those things for awhile, when cancer doesn't go away it makes your mom very sick and tired. As the cancer gets worse, it will be very hard for her to do things she used to – like cooking your favorite meal or walking to your bedside to kiss you goodnight.

If your mom had cancer before, it's hard to understand why she has cancer again. Why can't cancer just leave like last time? If the cancer wasn't found soon enough, it's still hard to understand...why can't the doctors make it go away? Why does mom have to die? Those are all very hard questions.

You should ask all the questions that come to your mind, even though some questions don't have easy answers. Talking about cancer doesn't make it get worse. Not talking about it makes you worry more. You might even ask a question someone else wants to ask, but is too afraid or just doesn't know how!

Life is a Teacher

You learn a lot about life by the things you see and hear. You hear lots of adult sayings like "everything happens for a reason." Other adults say "God is in control." While others say "everyone dies sometime."

None of those sayings seem to make you feel any better about watching someone you love lose the battle with cancer; especially when that someone is your mom. You count on her for so many things. It's hard to imagine that she won't be there for those things. There may be some things that you haven't even thought of yet.

It's important to remember that nothing you did or didn't do caused your mom's cancer.

13

Life is a teacher. The older you get, the more you learn - about a lot of things! Think about when you've asked your mom questions and she always seemed to have the answer! She even seemed to know when you were doing something you weren't supposed to – it's like she had eyes in the back of her head!

Some of the things life teaches us feel good and other things feel bad. The annoying part is that you often don't get to choose what will be good and what will be bad. Cancer is one of those things that makes you feel bad.

You also don't get to choose how long someone lives. It's almost like a silent rule that moms are supposed to stick around and cancer can change that – that is NOT fair!

Yet, what you learn from the bad stuff matters more than the bad stuff itself. Going through bad stuff can teach you to be thankful for things and people. It can teach your family about faith and prayer; it can even help you believe in God more. The things you learn won't make losing your mom any easier, but the things you learn will definitely make you stronger. It's like that other saying adults have, "what doesn't break you, makes you stronger!"

Prized Possessions

Losing important things makes us really, really appreciate them. Losing a special toy or a pet can make you feel really bad. But finding them again can make you feel really good! It's sort of like that when people we love die. If you've ever lost a grandparent or family pet because they died, you know how much it hurts. You miss them A LOT! When someone you love dies, it really, really hurts because you know you won't see them again – it can feel like they're lost forever! Even though it's good to know they're in heaven, you still can't see them.

Remembering can help you with the hurt you're feeling, and help you cope with losing your mom. You can try to remember the things she said and did. You can try to remember the way she smelled and the way she laughed. You can remember her favorite color, her favorite movie, her favorite food and other favorite things. You can remember all these things, even after your mom dies.

17

18

Memories are prized possessions, things that are worth saving like keepsakes. Some kids save special toys or shiny, colorful rocks. Some kids save notes from friends or homework with an "A" marked on it. You can save lots of important things, especially memories. You can start saving "MOMORIES," these are things that remind you of your mom. MOMORIES are the kind of memories that are just between you and your mom!

You can even still save them after she's died because things you do and see will remind you of mom. So, it's okay to make new MOMORIES too. You should also keep doing some of the things you enjoy – like going to a movie, enjoying sports like surfing and spending time with friends. It will help you cope better when you do fun things from time to time.

Moms do some awesome things with their kids and there are pictures to prove it! You and your mom might share special words – like the way you say goodnight to each other or the way she writes your name on a note. Those things are MOMORIES to save too!

You can put all your MOMORIES into a special box. Then when you're done with all your homework and chores, you can look in that box. Looking in that special box will help you whenever you miss her and wish you could see her.

It's normal for some memories to fade over time, for both kids and adults. But if you put your MOMORIES into a special box, all those things will help you remember stuff about your mom forever! You can even start a journal and write about your mom – there is one at the end of this book! A journal is just like keeping a diary!

If your mom wore pink in her fight against breast cancer, you can keep that celebration too! Just wear pink – pink ribbons, pink shirts, pink socks, pink hats or pink bracelets. You can also take part in all kinds of special events, like rallies, races and walks, for families who have gone through any type of cancer. People wear lots of different color ribbons, like pink, green, orange, white and gray at those events; people can wear them anytime to remember their loved ones who fought cancer.

Grief Isn't Quick

When your Mom's cancer doesn't go away, she still might have some time left with you – it all depends on the type of cancer and when it's found. Waiting is very, very hard! Think about when you've taken a long trip – you ask over and over, "Are we there yet?" But you know that asking doesn't make it happen any faster!

Waiting for someone to die is a very different kind of waiting. It's a very sad kind of waiting. It becomes harder and harder and harder. Even your mom will probably get tired of waiting. She may start to talk about death a lot more. That's her way of accepting that dying is part of life – and a part that she now has to do. It's even okay for you to talk to your mom about dying, even if it feels really different or weird.

It's better to talk to your mom than to wonder about things. You may wonder about the medicines the doctors give her or why she even takes medicine – especially if the cancer isn't going away. Medicines are tricky that way; they help people get well and they help people cope with not getting well. You may wonder about why some people visit your mom and others don't. You may wonder about a lot of things.

23

It's important to know that sometimes your mom may be too tired to answer questions. You can still make a list of the things you wonder about though. Or you can ask someone who knows your mom really well, like your dad, grandma, aunt or close family friend. As

happy   sad   angry

the cancer gets worse for your mom, she'll sleep more and she may even say funny things as her mind gets tired too. Imagine when you're really tired and you can't help falling asleep because your eyes feel so heavy. After fighting for a long time your mom is really, really tired like that. When your mom gets that tired, it can be hard for everyone.

Some people may ask her to fight harder and take more medicines. Others may see that she's very tired and she's not getting any better. Still others who love your mom may get angry and stop talking.

scared

frustrated

confused

Everyone may cry a lot and that's okay. You know how mom says you need to get a shower so your body gets clean? Well, tears clean your body from the inside – deep down to the inside of your heart in fact! Grief can make people not laugh as much or want to spend time alone. That is what grief looks like – and waiting is very painful. Grief helps you cope with loss and death.

Saying Goodbye

How do you say goodbye to your mom when she's dying from cancer? You're probably used to saying goodbye when you go out with friends, when you go to school, or somewhere else without your mom. Now you must say goodbye in a very, very different way. You might hear adults say "God takes everyone in His time." And this is your mom's time.

You might wonder why you can't just go to heaven with your mom, where there is no more pain and no more tears – but it doesn't work that way. Some people live for a long, long time and other people die much earlier than expected. No one really understands God's reasons for that, but you can smile knowing that your mom is going to a place where there isn't any cancer.

You can say goodbye by hugging her and saying "I love you" and "I'll miss you so, so much." You can say goodbye by thanking your mom and telling her you won't forget her. You can say goodbye by celebrating her birthday – even if it's not really her birthday! You can celebrate early just for mom!

You can even say goodbye after she dies by praying. You don't need any fancy words to pray, just talk about whatever you're thinking – whatever's inside your heart. God's a really good listener and praying can help you get through hard times.

There isn't just one way to say goodbye and it's never easy. Whatever way you choose to say goodbye, remember that your mom loves you and she'll be thankful no matter how you do it! Some of your aunts, uncles, cousins and friends may not get to say goodbye like you can. They may live far away so they can't be with your family. Some may send their love through phone calls, cards, letters and packages. They may share favorite memories and talk about their love for your mom.

Sometimes people choose to say goodbye at a "memorial" service. Some people call that a "funeral" service. At services like that some people cry, some people look very, very serious, and some people laugh, while others just look confused and lost. That all might make you feel pretty helpless and sad—but you can help!

You can give out hugs to anyone you feel needs one. Hugs are like a very special kind of medicine because they make the person giving one and the person getting one feel better! You don't even have to say anything; a hug is like having a bunch of good-feeling words wrapped up in silence.

 28

30

After Death

It is good for families to talk about life and death. While we want the people we love to live a long, long time, that doesn't always happen. When cancer doesn't go away, you have to "get ready" for death. You might have even tried imagining your life after your mom dies, but it's hard to imagine until it really happens!

For months, maybe years, you and your family have taken care of your mom just about every day, being right near her as she fought cancer. Suddenly life may feel very empty. Mom is gone and cancer is gone. Visitors are gone. People around you have moved on with other things.

You might even feel like you dreamed it all, like it didn't really happen. Like you want to pinch yourself and yell "Mom" and she'll answer like she always did when you called her name. But it did happen; your mom did die. So how do you do the things you used to do – without her?

You have to. You have to do all the things she would have expected you to do. You go to school; you help around the house; you learn new things; you eat your veggies; you laugh and play; you cry when you feel like you need to and you hug your family and say "I love you."

You get on with living and everyone in your family needs to do their part too. It's painful because you miss her so, so, so much. Times like this, take out those MOMORIES. Remember the things you wrote and the things you saved in that special box? Enjoy all those things that help you remember and not miss her so much!

By choosing to remember those things, you are celebrating her life and you are also moving on with your life. At first that will be super hard, but it will get easier, promise! You might consider having a special celebration on mom's birthday. You can bring out the photo albums and share stories of mom. Everyone in the family will have different stories! You might even frame a favorite picture and keep it in a special place.

Don't forget to celebrate having new people in your life too. It's okay to have new people in your life because no one will ever take mom's place. Letting new people in your life makes life less lonely and more fun, like shopping with a new babysitter or going to a movie with a friend. That's an important part of moving on. Be sure to share the kind of love you'll always have for mom with other people. Love, hugs and prayers are really, really good things to share with others. When you share, you receive from others too; you don't want to miss out on that!

33

Collective Courage

Even when you decide to move on with life there will be tough days—the "unbrave days." Those are days that you just don't feel like going to school. You just don't feel like doing your chores. Your dad may not feel like going to work. Your sister may not feel like talking to her friend. Those are the days for "collective courage!"

Collective courage means that you get together as a family and talk about why you're feeling so unbrave. You might hold hands and pray for strength, to collect even more courage. At first, unbrave days might be about missing your mom. But after awhile those days might be about other things too. Unbrave days might come when you have a fight with a friend, when you fail a test you studied really hard for, or when you have to do something new and you're just not sure that you can.

The awesome thing about collective courage is that you don't have to be brave, or courageous, all by yourself. You can borrow courage from your family and they can borrow from you! Together, you can have more and more brave days. One day at a time, you'll feel less sad and more brave about moving on with life.

Amazingly, collective courage works outside your home too. If someone in your family is having a hard time you can get help from others. Grandparents, teachers, pastors, neighbors, uncles, aunts and friends—are all people you can go to for some extra collective courage!

TIPS TO HELP FAMILIES:

1. If there's time, ask mom if she would like to make a short movie. That way her family will never forget what she looks and sounds like!

2. You might help mom write a letter, to pass on her wisdom and love.

3. Everyday do what you can and strive to do what you can't. Be sure to let teachers and other important people (working with your children) know about mom's illness and death—so there is support beyond home too.

4. Enjoy something funny together everyday. Tell a joke, play a game, lie on the lawn at night and give the stars funny names. Use your imagination, and laugh!

5. Start hugging others until they let go, never let go first. It's fun to see how long each hug lasts!

6. Write a list of things other people can do to help. When they ask, you won't have to think, you can just let them pick from the list. And your friends will be blessed to help you!

7. Allow time to grieve. Remember that everyone grieves differently, some longer than others. Be patient with each other and get help from a friend or counselor if you need it.

8. Do something new together as a family, start a new tradition and keep precious old ones too.

9. Celebrate each other's brave days with a special dessert, an extra story at bedtime or a dance around the house! Being brave deserves extra attention! Remember, no one sits this one out!

10. Love each other through the rough spots and encourage each other in all good things.

READINGS AND RESOURCES

Helpful Reads:

• Buddy's Candle: For Anyone Who Has Ever Lost a Loved One by Bernie S. Siegel, MD
Illustrated by Mari Gayatri Stein

• Prescriptions for Living: Inspirational Lessons for a Joyful, Loving Life by Bernie S. Siegel, MD

• How it Feels When a Parent Dies by Jill Krementz

• It Helps to Have Friends: When Mom or Dad Has Cancer by the American Cancer Society

• Another Morning: Voices of Truth and Hope from Mothers with Cancer by Linda Bachman

• Life After Loss: A Practical Guide to Renewing Your Life After Experiencing Major Loss by Bob Deits, M.Th.

Helpful Sites:

• www.bcrfcure.org
• www.cancercareforkids.org
• www.kidskonnected.org
• www.cancer.gov
• www.kidscope.org

References used for this publication:

• www.cancer.gov
• NIV Topical Study Bible New International Version. Zondervan Bible Publishers.

JOURNAL

39

JOURNAL

Made in the USA
Charleston, SC
22 June 2012